Professor Lessor's Animals

by Michael Ellis

illustrated by Carol Nicklaus

Mc Graw Hill New York

Macmillan McGraw-Hill Farmington

Book Design and Production: Kirchoff/Wohlberg, Inc.
Illustration: Carol Nicklaus

Macmillan/McGraw-Hill

A Division of The McGraw·Hill Companies

Macmillan/McGraw-Hill
1221 Avenue of the Americas
New York, New York 10020

Printed in the United States of America

ISBN 0-02-182141-0/3, L.8

3 4 5 6 7 8 9 FED 02 01 00 99 98 97

Professor Lessor's Animals

by Michael Ellis

illustrated by Carol Nicklaus

MACMILLAN / McGRAW-HILL

Our third-grade class had a visitor the other day. His name was Professor Lessor. He was supposed to tell us all about animals. When our teacher introduced him, he started laughing.

"Oh, no!" he said. "I came to talk about Annie Mills, the circus clown. *Annie Mills,* not animals!"

We all looked very sad. Our afternoon was ruined.

"Oh, deary me," said the professor. "You really want to hear about animals. Well, I'll give it a try. Why not?"

There was a good reason why not. The professor told us a lot about animals. He told us some interesting facts, but some of the things he said were just not true. We called those things *nonfacts.*

Now read what Professor Lessor had to say. You may be able to spot some of the nonfacts he told us. (HINT: There is one nonfact for each of the four animals Professor Lessor discusses.)

"First of all, animals are furry things that can't talk. Oops. Fish are animals, too. They don't talk, and they aren't furry either! Oh, dear. This is not a good beginning. I think I will just tell you about four of my favorite animals.

"Sharks are very special—even though they aren't furry. Did you know that there are more than 300 kinds of sharks? Sharks live in oceans all over the world. Many kinds of sharks swim in warm waters. I can't blame them. I like to swim in warm water, too.

"I'll bet you think all sharks are big. Well, they aren't. The smallest shark is about 4 inches (10 centimeters) long. The whale shark is the biggest. It can grow to be 60 feet (18 meters) long. In fact, the whale shark is the biggest fish in the sea.

"My favorite sharks are the dangerous ones— the mako, the hammerhead, and the great white shark. These sharks will attack any person they see, at any time!

3

"Now, birds are not furry animals. They have feathers. I like them anyway—especially owls. They really give a hoot!

"Did you know that most owls sleep during the day, just as bats do? At night, they hunt mice and other small animals. Owls see well in the dark. That is because they have huge eyes. Owls also have excellent hearing. They are very good hunters. Owls are really very wise!

Here's a riddle for you. What does a bird have that no other animal has?

Are owls *really* wise?

I've seen pictures of owls. They *do* have big eyes.

4

"You may be surprised to know that I'm bats. Oops. I mean, I like bats. For one thing, bats are furry. Bats also help people by eating lots of insects. Lots! A bat can catch and eat 150 mosquitoes in 15 minutes.

"Bats sleep during the day. Because they hunt at night, they can't see their food. Instead, bats make a special sound as they fly. When the sound hits an insect, it bounces back to the bat. Listening to the sound helps bats find food. The sound also keeps them from bumping into things. That's lucky, because bats are completely blind.

The way bats use sound to locate things is called **echo-location.**

I think I've *heard* that bats make a special sound.

Are bats completely blind? I always thought bats could see.

5

"Now on to another favorite animal. It's big! It's furry. It's creepy! It's a spider! I am talking about the tarantula.

"Just how big are tarantulas? One in South America measured 10 inches (25 centimeters) across with its legs stretched out. The largest kind in the United States is about 5 inches (12½ centimeters) long.

"Tarantulas can live a long time, too. Some kinds in South America live as long as 20 years.

"Can you believe that tarantulas don't bite? Well, they don't. Spiders have no teeth. But they do have sharp claws that can pinch. Beware of a tarantula's pinch. It's deadly!"

Are tarantulas *really* dangerous?

6

Fact-Checking

Did you find the nonfacts in Professor Lessor's talk? If you're not sure, look at the selection again. Here's a clue—the professor's last statement about each of his favorite animals was untrue. The rest of his descriptions were true.

Dear Friend

Write to Professor Lessor or to a friend telling what you learned or enjoyed about his speech. Be sure to tell what the nonfacts were.

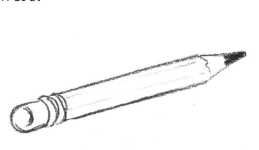

Animal Fact-ory

Now play the game "Animal Fact-ory." On the game board on the next page, you will find the nonfacts from the talk and the true explanations. You will also find some other facts and nonfacts.

Here's how to play.
- Use buttons or coins as markers.
- Roll the number cube. Move your marker.
- If you land on a fact or a nonfact, read it aloud. If you land on a square that tells you to do something, do it.
- You get 1 point for each nonfact you land on.
- You get 2 points for each fact.
- If you have to make a noise, tell a fact, or make up a nonfact, you get 3 points.
- Take turns.
- Play until one player reaches 20 points.

Now turn the page and play the game!

START

Make an animal noise.

Nonfact: TARANTULAS

A tarantula's pinch is deadly.

Fact: TARANTULAS

A tarantula's pinch may sting and cause swelling, but it is not deadly.

Make up a nonfact about an animal.

Nonfact: BATS

Bats are blind.

FINISH

Congratulations, you're now an animal expert!

Fact: TURTLES

A turtle's shell is part of its body. An empty shell means the turtle has died.

Nonfact: TURTLES

Turtles can walk out of their shells.

Fact: BATS

Bats can see about as well as people can.

Nonfact: OWLS

Owls are wise.

Fact: OWLS

For their size, owls have small brains. Their big eyes make them look wise.

ANIMAL FACT-ORY

Fact: SHARKS

Sharks don't even like the taste of humans. When they attack, it is usually a mistake.

Nonfact: SHARKS

Sharks will attack any person they see, at any time.

Fact: WHALES

Whales, like dolphins and porpoises, are not fish. They are mammals.

Nonfact: WHALES

Whales are the biggest fish in the sea.

Make up a nonfact about an animal.

Fact: OSTRICHES

Sometimes ostriches stretch out their necks to the ground to eat.

Nonfact: OSTRICHES

Ostriches hide their heads in the sand.

Tell a fact about an animal.

8